"We are living in unprecedented times when the walls of our physical homes are no longer the reliable boundaries they once were. Any stranger can enter our days through a direct message on social media. Our precious hours can be penetrated at any moment by a notification on our small screen, and these seemingly small encounters with others' energies impact our bodies and minds in powerful ways. Now more than ever, we need tools for managing those less visible borders between ourselves and our chaotic worlds, between our own healing paths and those that do not belong to us. To that end, Ora North's book is a timely and potent resource that will resonate across generat˙

—**Danielle Dulsky**, founder of The Hag Sch
The Holy Wild and *Bones and Honey*

T0271702

"Ora has offered us an apothecary of psychospiritual medicines to integrate into our unique healing paths.

If you're ready to level up your self-awareness, reclaim your emotional energy and personal power, and stand with clarity in the center of your own life, this book is for you. Ora speaks deeply to the empath's journey to wholeness, and her healing wisdom is needed now more than ever."

—**Pamela Kowal, MS**, marriage and family therapist emeritus, integrative psychotherapist, and soul mentor

"*The Empath's Guided Journal* is a book I wish I had been given in my teens, as it would have saved me many decades of heartache. The journaling prompts get right to the root of why life is often arduous for empaths. If you need help with an honest unravelling of the roadblocks to your healing, this book will be a breakthrough. Gift yourself this amazing book—and buy a few extra for the tenderhearted in your circle."

—**Trista Hendren**, founder of Girl God Books

"Ora North has created another gem of a book with *The Empath's Guided Journal*. She skillfully teaches us ways to manage our big feelings, heal up our inner wounds, examine our shadow self, and learn to set boundaries so that we can feel safe in the world. If you are an empath seeking to find your superpower, this journal is for you. Give yourself a gift and grab your copy today!"

—**Lisa Campion**, author of *The Art of Psychic Reiki* and *Energy Healing for Empaths*

The Empath's Guided Journal

YOUR SPACE TO SOOTHE EMOTIONAL OVERWHELM,
EXPLORE YOUR SHADOW SELF &
FIND BALANCE IN RELATIONSHIPS

ORA NORTH

REVEAL PRESS

AN IMPRINT OF NEW HARBINGER PUBLICATIONS

Publisher's Note

This publication is designed to provide accurate and authoritative information in regard to the subject matter covered. It is sold with the understanding that the publisher is not engaged in rendering psychological, financial, legal, or other professional services. If expert assistance or counseling is needed, the services of a competent professional should be sought.

NEW HARBINGER PUBLICATIONS is a registered trademark of New Harbinger Publications, Inc.

New Harbinger Publications is an employee-owned company.

Copyright © 2024 by Ora North
    Reveal Press
    An imprint of New Harbinger Publications, Inc.
    5720 Shattuck Avenue
    Oakland, CA 94609
    www.newharbinger.com

All Rights Reserved

Cover design by Sara Christian

Interior design by Amy Shoup

Acquired by Jennye Garibaldi

Edited by M. C. Calvi

Printed in the United States of America

26 25 24

10 9 8 7 6 5 4 3 2 1   First Printing

Contents

INTRODUCTION . . . 1

CHAPTER 1   Identifying as an Empath . . . 9

CHAPTER 2   Big Feelings . . . 23

CHAPTER 3   Core Wounds and Inner Children . . . 43

CHAPTER 4   Getting to Know Your Dark Side . . . 65

CHAPTER 5   Boundaries . . . 89

CHAPTER 6   Relationships . . . 119

CONCLUSION . . . 171

Introduction

"YOU'RE TOO SENSITIVE."

Maybe that's something you've heard before. Maybe you've heard it from friends, partners, family, or even strangers. You're too sensitive. But how can you be too much of something that makes you special?

Your sensitivity is a beautiful gift. You are more in tune with the subtle energies of nature and can appreciate the wisdom found there. You can find yourself in tears, in awe of a glorious sunset. You can appreciate art and music in such deep ways, they become entirely new worlds. You can easily share the joy of a friend, because their joy is your joy. You feel it in your body, in your bones. In fact, your ability to feel joy is altogether unmatched. What gives others happiness gives you pure ecstasy. Who would ever want to give up such a gift?

Unfortunately, that ability to go so high also inevitably brings you down very low. What gives others disappointment gives you heart-shattering pain. You can so easily feel pain, both in yourself and in others. If a loved one is suffering, you feel that suffering as if it were your very own. Sometimes you can feel it in your body, too. You can experience random physical symptoms and pain as an echo of someone else's. The pain of the world, and the pain of others, can become such an entangled part of you that you begin to confuse where you end and others begin. This is when you begin to understand why someone would say you're too this or too that—because you begin to agree with them, as you feel more and more overwhelmed. Suddenly, that beautiful sensitivity feels like a curse.

The truth about being so sensitive is that it is both a gift and a curse, but more than that, it simply is. We could spend our entire lives categorizing and labeling these qualities and aspects of ourselves as good or bad, but what's the point of that, unless we are figuring out how to manage the reality of what we are, regardless of its goodness or badness?

The sensitive empath is a lot of things, but put plainly, an empath is someone who simply takes in an excess amount of emotional information from themselves, others, and their environments. This means they can often feel the emotions of others, sniff out hidden motives, and experience different energetic layers in their environments and relationships. This is also why empaths are natural healers and caretakers—they are able to see and feel the places that need the healing and love in the first place.

Because there is always an excess of emotional information readily available to you as an empath, it is all too easy to get overstimulated and overwhelmed. This not only makes it impossible to do the kind of healing work you may want to do, but also can make even basic living difficult. Things become even more complicated if you have past trauma and wounding. Boundaries are difficult for empaths to develop at first, so you may have a tendency to blur what is yours vs. what is others' when it comes to trauma.

There is hope, though. There are ways to separate out what is yours vs. what is others', and there are ways to lessen that overwhelm. I want you to start thinking of your empath nature as a specific type of system. It is neither good nor bad, because that doesn't matter. It is simply the system you were given, and that system requires a specific type of care that is different from the needs and self-care of a lot of other people. You have to care for your unique system in unique ways, and your ability to do that relies on your willingness to understand yourself on the deepest levels possible. You must face yourself honestly and step into your own darkness, so you can truly understand how you exist in the world.

This guided journal will help you do just that. It will take you on a journey through your own experiences, feelings, and patterns, to help see you through the difficult parts of the empath experience.

First, you will reflect on your identity as an empath and examine the ways you've been expected to care for others more than yourself.

Next, you will dive into your big feelings. You'll learn to validate all of your emotions—not just the good ones—so you can better hold the entirety of your nature. You'll understand the ways you've been let down by others, or the ways you've let yourself down, all in the name of emotions. You'll see how those unexpressed feelings affect your physical and mental health. Using that awareness, you'll begin to build energy signatures, so you can identify and work with every single emotion you experience, including rage and grief. Not only will you work with each emotion, but you'll be able to recognize both sacred and harmful manifestations of those feelings, and begin to see how your trauma is interwoven into your emotional experience.

You'll recall the wounds of your inner child, so you can initiate new relationships with the younger pieces of yourself and incorporate reparenting practices to bring those pieces into wholeness.

Once you've built upon all of these layers, you'll be ready to take a dive into your dark side. You'll experience your victim and villain archetypes to get to know your shadow side, and see how our shadows are always at work in our lives and relationships. Knowing how your shadow side operates will allow you to give your shadow another job—one that doesn't involve ruining your life.

You can't get through the empath journey without stumbling in your relationships, so you will also be examining your relationships, the common energetic patterns you experience, and how to build and implement boundaries that are fluid and powerful.

The practices in this journal will help you organize all of that excess emotional information you receive and feel, so you can begin to understand better how your unique system operates. You will be creating order from chaos. Creating this kind of awareness and order is what helps establish new understandings and new habits that will make your life infinitely easier. You will be writing your way out of emotional overwhelm and into the life of an empowered empath.

These are exercises that I have personally been practicing, fine-tuning, and teaching for years. At one point in my life, I was the very essence of an overwhelmed empath. I was incredibly sensitive as a child. I felt more comfortable around the trees and rivers, and incredibly shy around other people. I couldn't name it at the time, but I was constantly feeling overstimulated by the energy and emotions of others. Feeling so much made me insecure and unable to express or process all of those feelings, especially since at the time, the empath identity wasn't mainstream, and no one around me could help me if they didn't even recognize what I was experiencing. I then experienced a lot of traumatic events that not only amplified my sensitivity, but also overwhelmed me to the point where I often exploded in anger and self-destructive habits. My shadow side was in control as both a response to and a coping mechanism for my trauma and empathy.

Through a series of intense spiritual awakenings, I went on a decade-long healing journey, where I developed these practices to heal myself. I was receiving support and training from other teachers and healers, but found that the spiritual community overall was not providing me with the deep transformation I was seeking. At that time, it was largely full of toxic positivity and spiritual bypassing that made it impossible for me to work on my shadow and trauma. Based on years of learning and experience working with myself and then with others, these simplified prompts are designed to help you dig into the core of your empath nature and work on your growth from the root.

While nothing is an instant cure-all, and no one can be guaranteed happiness, learning yourself and your sensitive system will give you a foundation of empowerment that can easily change your life. As an empowered empath, you will know yourself so well that it will be much easier to filter out the excess energy from others. You will have a solid grasp on your boundaries, which means you'll be less likely to fall into traps with others who would abuse you, hurt you, or even simply waste your time and energy. Having the language of the empowered empath naturally improves every relationship you have, because you can express yourself and your needs, understand how to better communicate with others, and quickly recognize when relationships have met their end. You'll be a master at regulating your emotions and environment. That doesn't mean that you won't continue experiencing the entire spectrum of emotions from yourself and others—rather, it means that you'll have tools and actionable tasks to find your own balance instead of being at the mercy of your reactions. All of these things create the space you need to examine and go after what you truly value in this life. Just imagine how much time and energy would be freed up for you if you weren't spending so much of it being overwhelmed or being tossed around in the waves of your environment and relationships. Imagine the peace you could feel if you knew you were living your purpose.

How to Use This Journal

This journal is best used daily or weekly while you are intentionally going on a healing journey for yourself. Some of the prompts or exercises take some time to ponder and act on, so certain sections may take longer than others.

It's also important to work on this not only when you are feeling good, but also when you're feeling triggered or overwhelmed. The kind of work we're doing here relies on your honesty with yourself, including about the more difficult aspects of yourself and your life experiences. The more honest you are, the more helpful information you'll be able to uncover and use for your transformation.

Because healing is a circular journey with many layers, you can return to each prompt multiple times and receive new understanding and wisdom. This will prove especially true as you continue to evolve on your journey as an empath. What is true for you in this moment, right now, may not be true for you in a couple months or a couple years. You will naturally graduate from exercises that seem life-changing right now, because you won't need them anymore. They will have already done their job. Others will be regulation practices that you will use again and again throughout your entire life.

You can also use this journal with others. I've often worked together with clients on these exact practices, and I've also had many readers who were referred to my work by their therapists. Having professional support is never a bad thing when working on personal growth. Having a book club or writing club where you can discuss the exercises and share what you've written in your respective journals is another great way to have support around the process.

One more way to use this journal is by using bibliomancy, a divination practice using books. You can do this by randomly turning to a page and seeing what prompt and theme the universe wants you to work on. When doing this, you'll often find that the results are very synchronistic with what-ever has been coming up for you in your life.

No matter how you end up using this journal, trust that your intuition is guiding you to the things that need your love and awareness. Trust that through even the simple process of opening your heart to the work here, transformation will follow.

CHAPTER 1

Identifying as an Empath

EVEN IF YOU ALREADY KNOW YOU'RE AN EMPATH, there may be some signs and symptoms of being an empath you haven't fully realized. Use this checklist to bring your awareness to the ins and outs of being an empath:

- You experience sensitivity toward other people.
- You can physically feel energy.
- You know things about others without being told.
- People, even strangers, tend to unload their life stories or secrets on you.
- Children and animals are naturally drawn toward you.
- You can tell when someone is lying.
- You are easily overwhelmed in crowds.
- You have food or chemical sensitivities.
- You are a healer or an aspiring healer.

- You have strong emotional reactions (good or bad) to movies, books, music, and other forms of art.

- You're drawn to nature.

- You need a lot of alone time to decompress and recharge.

- You had strained relationships with your parents.

- You tend to be creative or artistic.

- You experience strange pains in your body that may mimic the pain of another.

- You have bouts of tears or rage that may or may not be your own.

- You have accurate dreams about yourself, others, or events in your environment.

- You may have experience with toxic or abusive romantic relationships.

- You are a natural caretaker and somehow know another's needs without them telling you.

You'll notice that the above checklist contains both positive signs and negative ones. You already may have ideas or beliefs about whether being an empath is a positive or negative thing, especially considering that society often presents it as either an idealized or a demonized identity, but I want you to really consider both sides of the spectrum. Your sensitive system can experience a multitude of (sometimes contradictory) things.

In what ways has being an empath been a curse in your life?

_____

_____

_____

_____

_____

_____

In what ways has it been a gift or given you certain advantages?

_____

_____

_____

_____

_____

_____

_____

Your Empath Origins

Tracking your awareness and experience as an empath helps to lay the foundation for discovering which practices will be most important to you and how you can best serve yourself and your healing.

When did you first hear the term "empath" and how did it make you feel?

_____

_____

_____

_____

Looking back, what were the first signs or symptoms that made you feel like you were different from others?

_____

_____

_____

_____

_____

_____

_____

Around what age were you when those symptoms were becoming prominent for you? What was happening in your life?

What was your relationship to nature and animals when you were younger?

What is your relationship to nature and animals now?

Describe your physical environment growing up. Did you grow up in the city? The country? With a lot of other people, or a lot of time on your own?

_____

_____

_____

_____

Knowing what you know about yourself as an empath so far, how do you think the environment of your upbringing affected those signs and symptoms?

_____

_____

_____

_____

_____

_____

_____

_____

At what point did you realize that you were overwhelmed by emotions? Was there a specific instance? When was it?

Remember your answers as you continue on. You may find that your reflection on your environment ends up being a missing link in your healing, or that the simple choice of where you live may actually be helping or hindering you in a way you haven't fully realized. You may even be tripping over triggers from your younger years that were so normalized that you don't realize they're still sabotaging you.

Empaths and Others

A lot of the signs of being an empath are focused on others. How you experience others or help others can become the overarching theme of your empath experience, especially if you're drawn to helper roles like healer, therapist, teacher, social worker, or parent. And while the ability and willingness to serve others is incredibly important, it can cause you to lose your independent identity.

In what ways is your empath nature used to serve and help others?

_____

_____

_____

_____

If you took away your roles that are focused on helping others, what roles are left? Who are you when you're not serving others?

_____

_____

_____

_____

_____

_____

Just because you can help, doesn't mean you always should. When you continuously give, you'll find yourself trying to pour from an empty cup. Once your cup is empty, the drive to help others becomes harmful to you.

Can you think of an instance where your cup was empty, and you still pushed yourself to help? What happened, and how were you affected?

_____

_____

_____

_____

_____

Have you ever felt resentful while helping someone else? What were the circumstances?

_____

_____

_____

_____

_____

_____

Think about all the energy you spend focused on everyone else's problems. Imagine taking a portion of that energy out of those situations and redirecting it to taking care of yourself. What would that look like?

_____

_____

_____

_____

_____

How would your life look if you felt more consistently nourished and lived with a full cup?

_____

_____

_____

_____

Caring about others is a beautiful and noble way to live. The peace you feel when you do something kind for someone else, no matter the size of the gesture, is no small thing. However, continuously helping others when your cup is empty turns that peace and that kindness into something less. Those emotions can form into resentment instead, which is the slippery slope to empath martyrdom and disempowerment. When you include nourishing yourself on your list of priorities, not only will you be willing and able to help others, but you'll also feel good about it.

Empaths as Artists

In the same way that a painter paints and a writer writes, an empath feels. The act of feeling, for an empath, is not just a by-product of or a way to serve other people, but a solitary art. The empath is not just a sponge for other people. The empath is a solitary artist. The sheer amount of raw power and emotion that is available to you as an empath because of this is so intense that you need creative outlets to channel it. You can't simply let those energies sit inside you. Eventually, you'll feel both stagnant and overwhelmed at the same time. The ability to fully express creativity is a rare gift that must be explored, and with all the emotional information you have access to, the world can be an unending well of inspiration and creation if you let it.

How did you express creativity as a kid?

_____

_____

_____

_____

What creative practices or hobbies do you have now?

_____

_____

_____

What does it feel like when you're in creative flow?

What does it feel like after you've finished something creative?

Are there creative hobbies that you've given up that you would like to get back to? Or new ones you really want to try?

What are the obstacles to you dedicating more energy to creativity, and how can you address them?

Have you monetized any of your creative hobbies? If so, has that changed your relationship to your creativity?

_____

_____

_____

_____

_____

Because of your sensitive system, you might experience that weird sensation of being "too full" in your head, even while being too tired in your body to keep a creative routine going. Getting started is the hardest part when you've been away from these practices for any length of time. But if you can train yourself to turn to your creative outlets regularly, you'll find that many of the energies that overwhelm or paralyze you will often sort themselves out when your creativity is flowing.

Also, keep in mind that if you have monetized any of your creative hobbies, their energy may now be tied up in the stressful energies of money and capitalism. There's absolutely nothing wrong with making a living from your creativity, especially if it brings you joy, but you'll simply want to be aware of those energetic connections. Those complications can create blocks or additional stress in your creative process, so building in extra practices to address that—or even developing a new creative outlet that is separate from income—will help keep the energy flowing.

CHAPTER 2

Big Feelings

BEING AN EMPATH MEANS EXPERIENCING BIG FEELINGS. Big pains, big joys—every feeling can seem magnified and amplified when you're a sensitive being. While there's absolutely nothing wrong with having big feelings, we live in a culture that doesn't quite understand the importance and validity of emotions. Many of us have been socialized to repress or hide our feelings, especially the negative ones. Happiness is idealized while pain is demonized, creating a pressure cooker: we are constantly trying to hide our pain while pretending our happiness always prevails. This process of repression becomes normalized the longer you do it, and you may not even realize how many emotions and how much energy you haven't been allowed to express.

Being an empowered empath, however, requires that we witness and validate all of our feelings. Even and especially the ones we consider bad. Building and allowing this awareness paves the way for healthy expression.

In what ways have others asked you to bypass or repress your own feelings? Think about many different time periods, from childhood to now.

_____

_____

_____

_____

_____

_____

_____

In what ways have you asked *yourself* to bypass your own feelings?

_____

_____

_____

_____

_____

_____

_____

You deal with so much emotional information as an empath, and whenever you repress or bypass your own feelings, you're creating an excess of emotional information in your mind and body. That energy doesn't simply go away, and when you, as a sensitive person, don't address that excess, it can filter itself into your physical body and your nervous system. Your cells will hold onto it and create physical symptoms and pains because of it. You can even make yourself sick. Discovering where you're holding excess energy can help you begin clearing it.

What does it feel like in your body when you or others bypass or reject your feelings?

Where in your body can you still feel that rejection? Describe the location and sensation. Does it change or intensify when you focus on that feeling?

Have you experienced any physical chronic symptoms that are connected to these locations or sensations?

_____

_____

_____

_____

_____

All of the excess energy in your nervous system can also impact your mental health, interrupting the way your brain processes your experiences.

How is your mental health impacted when you're feeling emotionally overwhelmed?

_____

_____

_____

_____

_____

Are there any experiences you didn't get to have or experiences that were ruined or interrupted because of that overwhelm and overstimulation? (Think travel, concerts, dates, any other joyful experiences.)

How would your life be different if you didn't experience those interruptions?

Energetic Signatures

Every emotion has its own energetic signature—like a unique barcode—which can help you easily identify and work with it. Building an energetic signature for each emotion helps you organize all of the emotional information you process. And once those are in place, it makes it easier for you to give each emotion a job—or a way to express itself—since each emotion has a message for you.

 EXERCISE: BUILDING YOUR ENERGETIC SIGNATURES

To create a set of energetic signatures, pick three emotions, preferably including one or two negative emotions that come up frequently for you. Start with one of these feelings and allow yourself to sink into it. Breathe deeply, close your eyes, experience the energy of that feeling, and then describe it. What color is it? What does it look like? Does it have a texture? What images do you see? Is it a person? An object? Where does that feeling live? Let it become a personality, someone you can get to know. Be honest about your feelings.

Here is an example for sadness:

Sadness is a dark gray-blue, like the color of the ocean on a gloomy day. Sometimes it's all-consuming, like the tide rushing in during a hurricane. Other times, it's calmly in the background, like still waters disappearing on the horizon. It's an ache in my chest, slowly flooding my heart until I have no choice but to empty it out through my tears. Sadness lives there, heavy in my chest.

FEELING: _____

ENERGETIC SIGNATURE: _____

_____

_____

_____

FEELING: _____

ENERGETIC SIGNATURE: _____

_____

_____

_____

FEELING: _____

ENERGETIC SIGNATURE: _____

_____

_____

_____

Just because an emotion may be considered negative, that doesn't mean it can't have a positive impact. Every emotion, regardless of what it is, can have both a sacred manifestation and a harmful manifestation.

Let's use sadness as an example again:

For me, sacred sadness is pure beauty and art. A melody composed through tears. A poem about the experience of life that is painstakingly lovely and honest. A philosophy book. An expression of yourself. Your version of sacred sadness may be the same, or it may not—after all, there are so many different places that one can find the sacred.

Harmful sadness is perpetual drowning. It's hitting the snooze button on my alarm twelve times too many. It's watching too many sad movies and listening to too many sad songs. It's the slow sink into depression.

Sadness sends the message that I've seen too much and my sensitivities have been activated. It warns me that my attention is required, so that the sadness doesn't slip too far and become depression, and it wants me to deal with the less-than-perfect realities I've seen. It wants me to open myself further to the small joys in life and in my loved ones, so I can meet my sadness with love and compassion. It wants me to ask for help from my support system.

Consider one of the feelings you've been exploring. What are some of the ways that feeling can have sacred manifestations?

What are some of the ways that feeling can have harmful manifestations?

_____

_____

_____

_____

_____

_____

_____

_____

What is the message your emotion is sending?

_____

_____

_____

_____

_____

Rage

While it often has a bad reputation, rage is the mother of boundaries and justice. Rage usually sends the message that your boundaries, or the boundaries of your loved ones, have been crossed. It tells you that active change is required to rectify the situation. Rage is often a reaction to injustice in the world. While most of us have been conditioned to either repress rage and act like it doesn't exist, or redirect it in an unhealthy way that ends up hurting others, rage is the fuel that pushes you to do something about injustice or trespass. Rage is one of the most important and powerful emotions you can feel.

Describe a time in your life when you felt rage. What were the circumstances and what was the root cause of that rage?

Looking back on that time, can you see how that rage may have had a sacred purpose? What was that purpose?

What was the response—from both yourself and others—when you experienced that rage? Did your rage feel welcomed or rejected?

In what ways have you repressed your rage? Why?

Why does the world need your rage?

Grief

Grief is arguably one of the most human things we can experience. It is one of the purest forms of love and compassion. Grief is our response to the impermanence of life. Everything ends eventually. Everything dies eventually. We grieve everything from the loss of loved ones to the loss of jobs to the loss of different phases or identities of our lives as we evolve. By allowing yourself to feel and honor your grief, you are consciously interacting with the greatest lessons of life. If you can face that kind of pain without turning away or repressing it, you are transcending one of the great cultural downfalls of our time and experiencing life in a deeper way.

Describe a time in your life when you felt grief. What were the circumstances and what was the root cause of that grief?

At the time, did your grief feel welcomed or rejected? Why?

_____

_____

_____

_____

_____

_____

_____

Describe the different types of grief you have experienced.

_____

_____

_____

_____

_____

_____

_____

_____

In what ways have you repressed that grief, whether because of yourself or others?

_____

_____

_____

_____

_____

What has your grief taught you?

_____

_____

_____

_____

_____

_____

Because empaths experience feelings so intensely, you may find that you can become a sponge for trauma. Maybe you've collected it without knowing it, storing your trauma or even the trauma of other people in your body and mind. Such experiences can often change who you are, and there is often a lot of grief to process before you can integrate those experiences.

How has your trauma, your own brokenness, made you who you are today, for better or worse?

_____

_____

_____

_____

_____

_____

_____

_____

_____

_____

_____

_____

_____

_____

_____

_____

Whenever you experience trauma or growth, setbacks or successes, you change. And whether that change is bad or good in your eyes, there are pieces of you, versions of you, that die as a result. Mourning those pieces of yourself and engaging with those losses is necessary so you can move on with clearer energy.

EXERCISE: MOURNING YOUR PAST

Choose a version of yourself, whether an actual version of you in the past or even a hypothetical version of yourself in the future whom you'll never be, and write an obituary for them. Write as many obituaries for as many versions of yourself as you need to.

_____

_____

_____

_____

_____

_____

_____

_____

_____

EXERCISE: WRITING TO YOUR FUTURE

Think of everything you've learned about yourself in your journey as an empath. Every loss you've experienced has also opened you up to a bigger and more expansive future. Write yourself a letter with your wishes and hopes for your future as a way to honor your past.

CHAPTER 3

Core Wounds and Inner Children

THERE IS A COMMON THREAD THAT WEAVES THROUGH MOST EMPATHS who are going through the healing process: the shared experience of feeling rejected for your sensitivity. The feeling that you do not fit into this world because you are too fragile, too emotional, or not tough enough. And though this is often a wound that occurs over and over throughout your life, there is also often a singular event from your younger years that got the whole ball rolling. This is called your core wound, and you can often trace many pains back to this one pain. It might be a traumatic event, but it could also be a small event that would seem unlikely to create such a wound. The actual event isn't as important as the emotional experience that made you feel like you didn't belong.

There are many people who don't remember their childhoods very well or can't think of a singular event that far back. That's perfectly okay. Because your pains are all connected and all attached to similar threads leading back to the core wound, if you pick a singular event that was more recent but still encompassed that emotion of feeling rejected for your sensitivity, the exercise still works.

EXERCISE: UNCOVERING YOUR CORE WOUND

Working with the core wound is an important step for the empath on their way to empowerment. Examining when and how your sensitive system first went sideways gives you the perfect opportunity to return to those pieces of yourself and provide them with the love and support they needed, which will nourish your present self to the point where you find yourself feeling different and making more empowered choices for yourself.

CAN YOU REMEMBER THE FIRST TIME YOU FELT REJECTED FOR YOUR SENSITIVITY OR WERE MADE TO FEEL BAD FOR YOUR EMOTIONS? HOW OLD WERE YOU? WHO MADE YOU FEEL THIS WAY?

WHAT WAS THE SCENARIO AND WHERE WERE YOU?

_____

_____

_____

_____

HOW DID THIS EVENT CHANGE YOU?

_____

_____

_____

_____

_____

_____

_____

_____

_____

_____

_____

_____

Exile and Home

Your core wound creates an emotional foundation built on exile rather than on acceptance and love. Whatever you experience after this core wound either affirms or denies that experience. If you had a loving family who nurtured your sensitivity to the best of their abilities, it may have soothed and healed that core wound to the point where it doesn't play as much of a role in your healing. However, if you grew up in an environment that didn't know how to nurture your unique sensitivity, you may have experienced more and more rejection that simply built upon the same foundation of exile, creating an even larger wound.

How did your environment and your upbringing affect your core wound or your sensitive nature?

Who were the main figures in your upbringing that made you feel rejected for your sensitivity?

_____

_____

_____

_____

_____

_____

_____

Who were the main figures in your upbringing that tried their best to nurture and love you for who you are?

_____

_____

_____

_____

_____

_____

_____

What patterns have been established as a result of your sensitivity being rejected? For example, maybe you've developed a pattern of avoiding intimacy with others for fear of being rejected. Or maybe you have a pattern of assuming your loved ones are rejecting you whenever a triggering event or phrase comes up for you, even if that's not their intention.

Most empaths feel like they don't belong in the world because of this rejection. Living in a world that wasn't meant for sensitive creatures and operates on systems that run counter to the empath experience only exacerbates any exile that was felt in the younger years.

In what ways do you feel exiled in the world?

_____

_____

_____

_____

What gifts do you have that you feel are not nurtured by our society or systems?

_____

_____

_____

_____

When do you feel the loneliest?

_____

_____

_____

_____

If there is one thing that we all crave, it's home. Not necessarily a specific house or a specific location, but the feeling of home. The feeling that you belong and that you are safe and loved for who you are. If you have a history of exile, the longing for home can be absolutely devastating. The home wound is incredibly important to understand as an empath, not only because it is tied to your core wound, but also because you are more likely to make questionable decisions in your efforts to find a home as a result of that core wound.

If the core wound is the problem, home is often the perceived answer. But when our core wounds are not being consciously worked with, we're more likely to fall into bad situations like cults, abusive relationships, dysfunctional families, and toxic jobs. Our desperation to feel like we belong is a powerful subconscious drive, and sometimes others will manipulate that desperation. Understanding your relationship to your pain and your longing will keep you so connected to yourself that you will naturally start making empowered choices that prioritize your own self-work and safety.

How would you describe the feeling of home that you long for?

Have you ever felt that sense of home, whether in a physical place or relationship or community? Are you still in it? If not, how did it end?

_____

_____

_____

_____

Describe a time when you entered into or held on to an unhealthy relationship because of that longing for home? It could be romantic, friendship, family, community, or something else entirely.

_____

_____

_____

_____

Have you ever felt manipulated or taken advantage of because of your loyalty to a cause/group/relationship?

_____

_____

_____

_____

The key to empowerment and protection is to take away the charge of desperation in ourselves so we can't easily be manipulated or hurt. If you know your core wound and your home wound, you're armed with a knowledge that is both soothing and regulating to your sensitive system. What's more, if you know the ways in which you feel exiled or desperate for home, you can examine the things or circumstances that you need to feel more at home, and practice providing them for yourself.

What are some ways that you can engage with those feelings of longing and meet some of the needs that spring from them?

Soul Loss and Inner Children

When we experience loss or trauma or rejection, we often experience what is called soul loss. Soul loss happens when, in response to a trauma or rejection, a piece of the soul fractures and breaks off to protect itself from that trauma. It's like a form of intentional dissociation. If your soul can more or less put away pieces of you that are experiencing a lot of pain, then you won't have to fully experience that pain. Soul loss can happen with all sorts of events at all different ages, and we have all had pieces of ourselves break off at many different points in our lives. If you think back to your core wound, that is one event where soul loss occurred.

You could live your entire life without those pieces of yourself. The pieces of your soul that fracture, however, contain a vital energy that you need to consciously reclaim at some point, in order to experience the best life possible. Those wounds are frozen in time, preventing you from experiencing the joy that comes from healing them. Those wounds could be the reason you don't have successful relationships or aren't able to follow your dreams. If you feel like there's just something missing in your life, or like you're just not fully yourself, those are signs that you're ready to address your soul loss and rediscover those pieces of yourself.

To reclaim these lost pieces, you need to acknowledge them as they were when they broke off and begin a relationship to integrate them back into your life. You need to acknowledge and work with your lost pieces that way because they are frozen at the age, emotions, and environment that they were experiencing when they parted from you. They did not grow or evolve, so you need to meet them where they are. Many of these pieces, including the one from your core wound, are your inner children. Being able to reclaim the inner children that were separated from you due to soul loss can reinfuse your life with joy, meaning, and purpose.

To reclaim your inner children, you need to give them what they needed then, now. By figuring out who your inner child was at the time of your core wound, you can begin to understand what they need to be reintegrated into you.

Describe the personality of your inner child from your core wound. What did they like, dislike? What were their favorite things to wear, to do, to eat?

EXERCISE: A DAY WITH YOUR INNER CHILD

Choosing activities to do with your inner child—specifically for your inner child—is what creates and improves the relationship. For example, my inner child is an animal lover. Spending time with and caring for animals was her favorite thing to do. When I was embarking on my own deep soul healing journey, I got a puppy for my inner child. Having that puppy to take care of was the most healing and most fun thing I ever did for my inner child, or let my inner child do, and that process reintegrated that lost piece of my soul. Other examples of activities for your inner children can include coloring or art, watching certain movies you loved at the time of the soul loss, going to museums, buying stuffed animals, wearing your inner child's favorite color, or skipping rocks at the lake. The possibilities are endless—you just need to discover what your inner child needs.

PLAN A DAY FOR YOURSELF AND YOUR INNER CHILD. WHAT ACTIVITIES WOULD YOU CHOOSE?

Not only can you provide your inner child with activities that will make them feel safer with you, but you can also meet the physical and emotional needs that they didn't have fulfilled at the time of the soul loss. For example, if your inner child was not fed properly, then indulging in delicious food or learning to cook would be incredibly helpful for reintegration. Maybe you never got a good night's sleep because of family drama and anxiety. In that case, your inner child might love a good sleep routine, complete with beautiful bedding, pillow mist, and a white noise machine. Or, if your inner child felt as though they weren't allowed to express themselves, then practices of expression like singing or speaking will be especially healing for you.

One of my more eccentric practices is going out into the woods alone and talking out loud to the trees, because my inner child loves nature and also feels the need to be heard. This is a practice in self-witnessing and self-validating, and every time I do it, I'm still surprised by how helpful it is.

What did your inner child need at the time of the soul loss, both physically and emotionally?

How can you give your inner child those things now?

_____

_____

_____

_____

_____

_____

_____

_____

_____

_____

Above all else, your inner child needs to feel safe with you, and they need to be having fun. Joy is the secret ingredient to most magical and healing work, and getting in touch with the things that bring your inner children joy is what encourages them to stay and integrate into you again. Healing work can be very heavy, and joy and fun are what create long-term results.

Mother and Father Wounds

Most of us have both mother wounds and father wounds, or wounds from our parental figures that impacted our development and personalities as adults. Mother wounds are often associated with emotional nurturing and compassion, while father wounds are often associated with stability and material sustainability. Of course, not everyone had traditional parental roles in their childhood, so you may find that your parental wounds are a mix of various roles and energies. Exploring these roles will help you figure out how to meet your own needs using the healing technique known commonly as "reparenting yourself."

Reparenting yourself involves working with your inner child to discover which needs were not met by your parental figures when you were younger. Once you discover these needs and start to work on having a relationship with your inner child, you can further your healing by satisfying for yourself the specific needs that your parents didn't meet. It also involves getting honest with yourself about the ways that your parents harmed you, whether consciously or unconsciously on their part.

Describe your mother or mother figure(s) in your life. How did that relationship (or lack of one) create your mother wound?

What negative habits or patterns do you still find in your life because of that wound?

Describe your father or father figure(s) in your life. How did that relationship (or lack of one) create your father wound?

What negative habits or patterns do you still find in your life because of that wound?

EXERCISE: LEARNING HOW TO REPARENT YOURSELF

To reparent yourself, you have to step up, despite the longing for someone to fill that parental role, and take actions to mother and father yourself. In those difficult moments where all you can think is "I wish my mother could do this for me," you need to then turn inward, toward yourself, and ask, "How can I do this for myself? How can I mother myself?" Examples can be anything from giving yourself advice you'd wished your mother had given you to scheduling time off for a movie or a bath to comfort yourself.

WHAT ARE SOME THINGS YOU CAN DO TO MOTHER YOURSELF? WHAT CAN YOU PROVIDE FOR YOURSELF THAT YOUR MOTHER DID NOT?

_____

_____

_____

_____

WHAT ARE SOME THINGS YOU CAN DO TO FATHER YOURSELF? WHAT CAN YOU PROVIDE FOR YOURSELF THAT YOUR FATHER DID NOT?

_____

_____

_____

_____

Stopping negative family patterns is a very important practice for empaths. Even though you are conditioned to take on whatever has been passed down to you—both in genetics and in life choices—you have to make the choices that both empower your lineage and cut ties with the harmful aspects of it. Because you experience things even more intensely as an empath, that makes you both more susceptible to the harm in your lineage and more powerful in the strengths. Taking an inventory of these familial patterns and making decisions to support yourself accordingly is one of the keys to moving from a victimized or traumatized empath to an empowered one.

What are some of the negative family patterns in your lineage that have been passed to you? This could be anything from alcoholism to anger to abandonment to having a bad knee.

What decisions can you make in your life to stop those cycles?

What are some of the positive family patterns in your lineage that have been passed to you? This could be anything from open communication to physical longevity to kindness to having pretty eyes.

_____

_____

_____

_____

What decisions can you make in your life to honor those things and build them up?

_____

_____

_____

_____

_____

_____

_____

_____

Think about what you are passing down. Regardless of whether you have children or not, you are still passing an energetic lineage on to others. What is it that you want to leave with others? What is your desired energetic lineage?

CHAPTER 4

Getting to Know Your Dark Side

IT WAS THE FAMOUS SWISS PSYCHIATRIST AND PSYCHOANALYST CARL JUNG who developed the concept of the shadow archetype, which he described as "the unconscious aspect of the personality which the conscious ego does not identify in itself." Basically, your shadow is made up of the parts of you that aren't as desirable as the "good" parts. It's your dark side, and it's likely that you've been taught that your dark side must be rejected or ignored completely.

Carl Jung also described the shadow self as "the seat of creativity." He believed the shadow encompassed not only the unconscious negative parts, but also the unconscious positive parts. Some of our greatest gifts and greatest strengths can only be discovered when we willingly uncover our weakness and pain first.

While it's important for everyone to work with their shadow selves, it's especially important for empaths who are on the healing journey. Because empaths are feelers—they feel everything—they need to be able to work with every aspect and every feeling, not just the good ones. If you were to ignore your shadow side, you'd also be ignoring all of the hidden strengths in your pain.

Victims and Villains

An easy way to get to know your shadow side is by exploring your victim and villain archetypes. We all have these archetypes—versions of ourselves that amplify our darker traits. Your victim is the side of you that contains all the bad things that others have done to you. It could also be called your innocent self. Your villain, on the other hand, is the side of you that contains all the bad things you've done to others. This is an oversimplification, of course, but it gives you a good place to start.

Both of these archetypes need focused attention and creative expression, whether it's through an honest conversation with a friend, an art or writing project, music and dance, or any other form of expression that feels good to you. If they don't receive this kind of attention, these archetypes will find ways to seep into your life and express themselves in more damaging ways. They are usually responsible for broken relationships, self-destruction, self-sabotage, and negative spirals. Putting them to work through creativity, however, redirects that intense energy into projects that feed your soul rather than destroy your life.

EXERCISE: DESCRIBING YOUR INNER VICTIM

Think about your inner victim, the piece of you that contains all the bad things others have done to you. Use this space to describe your inner victim archetype. You can write a description or draw a picture—however this part of you wants to be expressed.

Knowing more about your victim now, describe ways that they have created pain or self-sabotage in your life. For example, if your victim was abandoned or treated badly, you may assume that everyone is going to leave you or treat you badly, which ends up preventing you from truly letting anyone in. Other examples of victim patterns are disempowerment, anxious behaviors, poor boundaries or communication, shutting down when confronted, and allowing yourself to continue being treated a way you don't like.

The victim archetype, or innocent, is often indicative of where your innocence was taken away. In what ways was your innocence taken away, and how
does that make you feel?

_____

_____

_____

_____

_____

_____

_____

The strange part about experiencing your victim archetype is that most
spiritual communities would argue that you should avoid being in victim
energy at all costs. They may tell you that you are perpetuating the energy.
But I've found that if your victim behavior keeps coming up, it actually means
that you haven't spent enough conscious time with it. Whether you are
screaming "I am not a victim!" or "I am a victim!," you may still be acting out
as your victim archetype either way—but you're not truly witnessing it on the
level it needs.

Once you fully allow yourself to acknowledge and process your own vic-
timhood, it will shift and transform on its own. Your victim tells you where
you need to give yourself more love and attention. This archetype is also
connected to your inner child, so a lot of the work you do for your inner child
will cross over into your victim expression.

EXERCISE: WORKING WITH YOUR INNER VICTIM

List five ways you can creatively express your victim side without causing harm. Some examples: inner child exercises, conversations with friends where you vent everything without judgment or correction, watching a sad movie that you relate to, playing music, and more inner child exercises.

1.

2.

3.

4.

5.

MUSIC IS A REALLY POWERFUL WAY TO CONNECT TO YOUR INNER ARCHETYPES. CREATE A MUSIC PLAYLIST FOR YOUR VICTIM THAT YOU CAN LISTEN TO OR DANCE TO. FIND SONGS THAT MATCH YOUR INNER VICTIM.

-
-
-
-
-
-
-

EXERCISE: DESCRIBING YOUR INNER VILLAIN

Think about your inner villain, the piece of you that contains all of the bad things you've done to others. Use this space to describe your inner villain archetype. You can write, draw—however these parts of you want to be expressed.

Your villain shows you how you protect yourself and process your rage. Your villain is often in charge of protecting your victim, so that nothing bad can happen to them again. Describe some ways in which your villain has protected you and your victim.

Knowing more about your villain now, describe ways that they have created pain or self-sabotage in your life. For example, your villain may have had to manipulate people or situations to stay safe, so maybe you still manipulate people or situations even when it's hurtful to yourself or others. Other examples of villain patterns are lying, hyperindependence, using sexuality in a way that may be harmful (this crosses over into the femme fatale archetype, which is common), poor boundaries or communication, avoidant behaviors, and treating others in ways that they don't like.

Since your villain is your protector, you can give them a new job instead of wreaking havoc. One thing to remember about your villain is that they are really into control. Whereas your victim gives up control, your villain takes it. The villain also adores creativity, so turning to creative pursuits is your best way to give your villain some time on stage without letting them run the show. Think of them as a performer or a storyteller.

EXERCISE: **WORKING WITH YOUR INNER VILLAIN**

List five ways you can creatively express your villain side without causing harm. Some examples: writing dark fiction where you can play out those villain tendencies in your characters, dancing, sexual practices like BDSM (Bondage, Dominance, Sadism, and Masochism), dressing up in costumes that express your villain, and shows or movies that match that energy.

1. _____

2. _____

3. _____

4. _____

5. _____

CREATE A MUSIC PLAYLIST FOR YOUR VILLAIN THAT YOU CAN LISTEN TO OR DANCE TO (ESPECIALLY WHILE WEARING YOUR VILLAIN OUTFIT).

- _____
- _____
- _____
- _____
- _____
- _____

Part of embracing your inner victim and villain is knowing that you will sometimes play a victim or a villain to someone else in their own story, and you have to learn to accept that rather than falling into a people-pleasing pattern or demonizing the other person. They have their own archetypes they're grappling with that you have no control over. It's absolutely inevitable that you will be seen in these ways at times. The only thing you can do is look back and see how much of your shadow side was playing the role vs. how much of their own shadow side was placing you in the role.

Think of a time when you were the pitied victim in someone else's story. What happened and how did that make you feel?

Now that you understand your victim more, can you see your inner victim in that situation? How much of it was you willingly stepping into the role vs. others forcibly placing you in that role?

Think of a time when you were the villain in someone else's story. What happened and how did that make you feel?

_____

_____

_____

_____

_____

_____

Now that you understand your villain more, can you see your inner villain in that situation? How much of it was you willingly stepping into the role vs. others forcibly placing you in that role?

_____

_____

_____

_____

_____

_____

Triggers

Our shadow sides are often released when we get triggered. Triggers are a surefire way to expose where in our lives we still experience pain and anxiety, thereby also exposing where we still need more love and compassion. Being triggered often happens when someone brings up a pain point in conversation—maybe something that references a traumatic experience you have. And whether you want to or not, you react out of impulse with anger, anxiety, or fear. For example, let's say you were cheated on in a past relationship by someone you really trusted, and later, in a new relationship, your partner says something that your previous partner said. It could be potentially harmful, but it could also be innocuous. Either way, it illuminates your pain point, and suddenly you find yourself angry and panicking that your new partner is going to cause you the same kind of pain. Triggers happen because a wound has been activated, and your natural defenses want to prevent any more pain or damage to that wound. That's why you feel defensive.

What are some past painful experiences that you already know you still feel triggered by?

In what situations do you find yourself most triggered? Who are the people you tend to be triggered by/around?

_____

_____

_____

_____

_____

How do those situations expose where you are still wounded and need more love?

_____

_____

_____

_____

_____

Triggers can be caused by details in singular past events, or they can be caused by themes that are often found in your life and your relationships. Knowing which is which will not only help you address them, but also help you communicate with others about the help you need.

Do you have any detail triggers from singular events? If so, what are they? These could be certain songs, smells, words or phrases, and so forth.

_____

_____

_____

_____

Do you have any themes that continually trigger you? What are they? Examples include feeling abandoned, feeling alone or unheard, and being told not to express your emotions.

_____

_____

_____

_____

Knowing both your detail triggers and your theme triggers can be a game changer, because you are bringing your awareness into the raw emotional experience. If you already know your triggers, you can acknowledge them when they occur. And once you're aware of them, you can choose to not engage from a place of anxiety or anger. You can choose to take a step back. Maybe that means you stop a conversation and take some space for yourself, preventing yourself from saying something you'll regret. Maybe it means that you tell the other person about the trigger, so they can also change their behavior, and everyone can either take a step back or take a step toward each other with a new purpose.

Practicing that kind of communication is still hard in the heat of the moment, even when you're aware. Try practicing what you could say to another person who has triggered you.

_____

_____

_____

_____

_____

Triggers also work to pull you down into conditioned neural pathways in the brain, or directions that your brain has traversed over and over again, creating a worn and well-traveled path that leads to the same thoughts and feelings. We are creatures of habit, and if you have recurring trauma and wounding as an empath, these well-traveled pathways seem to be the path of least resistance. To break these patterns, you can work with your triggers to trace them back, and begin to create more loving pathways for yourself and others instead.

When you get triggered, name the feeling out loud. Write it down. Even if you know you're overreacting and it isn't the feeling you'll end up with, honor the emotion in its raw, reactive state by acknowledging it.

_____

Why do you feel this way? Explain the circumstances of what triggered you and who was involved.

Why did what the other person said or did bother you so much?

Why is it important for you to not feel this way? What pain do you avoid if you aren't triggered?

_____

_____

_____

What negative experience from your past did that feeling of being triggered bring you back to?

_____

_____

_____

_____

_____

How was this situation different from your previous pain? How was it the same?

_____

_____

_____

_____

How can you and the other person acknowledge and honor your experience?

_____

_____

_____

How can you honor the experience of the other person involved?

_____

_____

_____

By tracing your triggers back like this, you'll begin to illuminate their origins, both in your past and in your brain. You can validate your own experience while also creating space to make different choices with yourself and the people you care about. By using this process, you'll also begin to understand the trigger system more and more when others get triggered. When curiosity and compassion are injected into our triggers, it becomes much easier to defuse the energy and reapproach one another with more love and less anger.

People often say that we are all mirrors of each other—that we are all constantly offering other people reflections and wisdom and insight into what they are experiencing internally. While this is true, it is only a half-truth, for our shadow archetypes warp these mirrors into creepy, circus-style funhouse mirrors. The things we may be seeing in or experiencing from others, especially when triggered, are often distorted versions of one another. Our victim and villain archetypes are the ones who try to take the wheel when our intense emotions get triggered.

Think of a time you got into a big fight with a loved one. Can you recall the triggers experienced by both of you?

Thinking about your own trigger in that fight and tracing it back, was your reaction more in line with your victim archetype or your villain archetype?

Thinking about the triggers and behaviors of the other person, was their reaction more in line with their victim archetype or their villain archetype?

The victims and villains of everyone involved are all looking for screen time in the movie of your arguments. With all of these different aspects fighting for attention, it's no wonder that emotional arguments are chaotic and oftentimes damaging. Your archetypes will escalate the problem in order to demand more of the attention.

What would it look like for everyone to take a step back from their victim and villain archetypes during arguments? How would it change the results?

Shadow work is a combination of radical acceptance, radical self-responsibility, and a willingness to see as much of your complicated and paradoxical truth as possible. By getting to know your dark side, you're able to let even more light into your life.

List five reasons you're grateful for your shadow side.

1.

2.

3.

4.

5.

What are the beautiful things you've been able to let into your life as a result of your shadow?

How does your shadow make your light even brighter?

CHAPTER 5

Boundaries

WORKING WITH YOUR BOUNDARIES IS AN ABSOLUTE NECESSITY when you're an empath. Your sensitive nature makes you more susceptible to a lack of boundaries when you're overwhelmed, and creating healthy boundaries can be a difficult habit to form because of that. If there is one thing that immediately improves the quality of your life, though, it's good boundaries. Think of your boundaries as the negotiations and agreements for what you want most from life. The more you know yourself and your values, the easier it is to live the life you want.

What is your relationship to your boundaries like right now?

How would you like your relationship to your boundaries to change?

Ground Yourself

To be able to make good choices and work with our boundaries, we must first make sure that we feel grounded in our bodies. One of the dangers of working with all of these self-healing tools is that you can get so in your head that you start to feel disconnected from your body. Having so much energy in your head without that physical connection to your body creates extra anxiety and worry, which is counterproductive to your healing process. This is where grounding comes in.

Grounding, also called earthing, is when your energy connects to and interacts with the energies of the earth. By allowing your body to physically connect with the earth, you create balance and stability on both a physical and spiritual level, and can simultaneously help ease your own pain on each level. Some examples of grounding are simply putting your feet in the sand, going on a walk or hike, dancing, and working with your hands—anything that engages your body and allows it to connect to the physical world around you.

What are some of the ways that you already ground yourself? How often do you use them?

List some new ways to ground or be in your body that you can use while going through your healing process.

- _____

- _____

- _____

- _____

- _____

- _____

- _____

EXERCISE: HEALING THROUGH GROUNDING

*Here is an easy grounding exercise that you can use as
part of your grounding protocol.*

- **YOU NEED BARE FEET FOR THIS EXERCISE.** Find a spot outside that calls to you. Whether it's a beach, a forest, a grassy spot outside your apartment, it doesn't matter. If weather doesn't permit, you can still do this exercise inside with bare feet, but any opportunity to connect your skin to the earth makes a big difference.

- **STAND OR SIT WITH YOUR BARE FEET CONNECTING DIRECTLY INTO THE EARTH.** Begin by straightening your shoulders, closing your eyes, and taking a few very deep, very intentional breaths.

- **AS YOU ARE BREATHING AND YOUR FEET ARE ON THE GROUND, VISUALIZE THE NETWORK OF THE EARTH CONNECTING TO THE BOTTOMS OF YOUR FEET.** I like to visualize networks of tree roots as if they were brain synapses, lighting up and connecting with my feet. Your network may look totally different, which is perfectly fine.

- **ONCE YOU ARE CONNECTED TO THIS NETWORK, THE ENERGIES OF THE EARTH AND YOUR BODY DO THE WORK.** They are automatically taking the excess energy of your mind—the anxiety and overwhelm—and giving you the support of the earth. You can visualize your energy moving downward into the earth while the earth feeds you life-supporting energy. As you breathe, focus on the gratitude you feel for being with the earth in your body. Stay in this place as long as you like.

Even if you don't like working with a lot of guided visuals, simply spending time connected to the earth works its magic. Notice the feelings and sensations that come up for you during this exercise and afterward.

Once you are grounded, you are much more equipped to continue with your healing. Your head will be clearer, which will make your boundaries clearer as well.

The Spectrum of Boundaries

Boundaries can be difficult because they are not meant to stay the same at all times. Boundaries need to be flexible and adaptive as you go through your life. Just as your priorities, values, and goals shift and change as you grow, your boundaries need to do the same. Knowing that there is a spectrum of boundaries, and where you fall on that spectrum at any given time, will help you become more aware of your needs and adjust your approach.

One end of the spectrum is the "not enough" side. This is where your boundaries have been underutilized, because you haven't figured out where your boundaries need to be just yet. Being on this end of the spectrum will make you extra vulnerable to other people's energies. This can cause uncontrollable weepiness, powerlessness, and hyperfragility. This is where everyone crosses your boundaries all the time, leaving you exhausted and overwhelmed.

Where in your life do you feel like your boundaries fall on this "not enough" side of the spectrum?

_____

_____

Are there certain people or situations that seem to trigger this side of you more often than others? Who are they, and what are the circumstances?

_____

_____

_____

When you're triggered as a result of lower boundaries, it's because something that happened has activated a wound. Think back to your history and core wounds. How do those wounds cause your boundaries to be too weak or nonexistent?

_____

_____

_____

_____

_____

In trying to be open or helpful, or simply being too overwhelmed to deal with boundaries, you've probably let in certain people or situations that ended up being really hurtful to you. Describe a scenario when you let in someone or something that wasn't good for you.

_____

_____

_____

_____

While you can't change the past, how can you change the way you look at your boundaries in the future when you feel like you're letting in something that isn't good for you?

_____

_____

_____

_____

_____

_____

_____

On the other end of the spectrum is the "too much" side. This is where you land when you've attempted to create firm boundaries for yourself, and by trying to protect yourself, you've built solid steel walls instead of flexible boundaries. Being on this end keeps the bad out, but it keeps the good out, too. This end of the spectrum will keep you invulnerable to others, but it also leaves you lonely. You may find yourself out of touch with your own sense of compassion and empathy, and you may find that no one can truly reach you.

Where in your life do you feel like your boundaries fall on your "too much" side of the spectrum?

_____

_____

Are there certain people or situations that seem to trigger this side of you more often than others? Who are they, and what are the circumstances?

When you have overly rigid boundaries, it's a defense mechanism. You are trying to protect yourself from feeling pain again. Think back to your history and core wounds. What are you trying to protect yourself from?

In trying to protect yourself, you've probably pushed away people or situations that may have been great for you. Describe a scenario where you pushed away someone or something that you wish you could have let in.

_____

_____

_____

_____

_____

While you can't change the past, how can you change the way you look at your boundaries in the future when you feel that you've pushed away something you should have let in?

_____

_____

_____

_____

_____

_____

Expression

One of the reasons empaths often have trouble with their boundaries is because they often struggle to express themselves honestly. If you're a sensitive being who wants the best for others, it makes sense that you might put the needs of others first, forgoing your own needs or boundaries. Saying "no" might be one of the hardest things you've had to learn. The only way boundaries work, however, is when you are able to verbally express them to yourself and others. If you have the respect for yourself that it takes to be clear about your boundaries, you are teaching others how to respect them as well.

Is it difficult for you to say "no" when others ask you for help? How often do you generally say "yes" when your intuition says "no"? And how often do you generally say "no" when your intuition says "yes"?

Why is it difficult to follow your own intuition in these situations?

What are you afraid will happen if you put your own needs first and express that to others?

_____

_____

_____

_____

_____

Do you ever feel like you have a lump in your throat when you can't express something? Do you ever feel that constriction or discomfort? Your throat chakra, the energy center located right in the middle of your throat, is in charge of truth and expression. When we don't express ourselves with our voices, we get blocks in our throat chakras.

To clear those blockages, you have to—you guessed it—use your voice! Being able to verbally speak your truth—not just knowing it in your mind—is incredibly important. And even when you don't know exactly what you would say yet, practices like singing or reading books or poetry out loud are a great way to clear that energy.

What is the hardest part about using your voice and expressing yourself?

_____

_____

_____

_____

EXERCISE: SPEAKING UP

BRING YOUR AWARENESS TO YOUR THROAT CHAKRA AND NOTICE ANY WEIRD FEELINGS OF CONSTRICTION YOU HAVE. WHAT IS IT THAT NEEDS TO BE SAID RIGHT NOW THAT YOU HAVEN'T YET EXPRESSED? WRITE IT DOWN, AND THEN READ IT OUT LOUD AS WELL.

THINK BACK TO THE LAST SITUATION WHERE YOU WANTED TO EXPRESS YOURSELF BUT DIDN'T. BECAUSE YOU DID NOT EXPRESS YOURSELF, THAT ENERGY STAYED IN YOUR BODY, POTENTIALLY CREATING BLOCKS. WRITE DOWN WHAT YOU WISH YOU COULD HAVE SAID, AND THEN READ IT OUT LOUD TO RELEASE THE ENERGY. REALLY PUT YOUR FEELING INTO IT WHEN READING.

Think back to the last time you were upset that someone crossed your boundaries. What were the circumstances? Did the other person know your boundaries? Did you verbally express your boundaries in that situation? Describe what happened.

_____

_____

_____

_____

_____

Looking back now, how does that situation inform you about where you personally are with your boundaries and your ability to express them?

_____

_____

_____

_____

_____

_____

When you've already verbally expressed your boundaries, and someone is still disrespecting them, it can be easy to second guess yourself and let the behavior continue to avoid further conflict. What can you do when you've already expressed yourself and someone continues to push or disregard those boundaries?

Gifts and Martyrs

There are so many gifts that go along with being an empath, and many of those gifts affect the lives of others, even to the point where the empath may identify themself through the lens of others. You may feel pressured to constantly use your gifts for others, losing your own sense of self in the process.

Which gifts do you feel pressure to use or embody—whether that pressure is from you or from others—regardless of how much energy or time you have? (For example, maybe it's your ability to listen to others and make them feel seen and heard.)

Are there any gifts that you wish you didn't have to use, or that you wish others didn't rely on you so much for? Why?

What does it feel like when you overextend yourself using your gifts?

_____

_____

_____

_____

When empaths overextend themselves, their energy becomes too weakened to be able to care for themselves properly. The insistent urge to help can often mean you're trying to pour from an empty cup, and at some point, it doesn't help anyone anymore. That urge is often what leads to martyrdom. In the context of your empath nature, martyrdom is when you believe you must always sacrifice your own needs to fulfill the needs of others, whether they are asking you to or not.

In what ways have you been pushed into martyrdom by others in your life?

_____

_____

_____

_____

_____

_____

In what ways have you willingly pushed yourself into martyrdom?

How does playing the noble martyr end up hurting you?

How does playing the noble martyr end up hurting the people you're trying to help?

While service to others is important and noble, sliding into martyrdom territory is especially unhealthy for an empath, because it places their own sense of value and worth in the hands of others. You deserve to feel your worth and value on your own, separate from what you can do for others. By turning inward with support, self-care, and creative expression, you'll be able to keep from overextending yourself into martyrdom.

Imagine you didn't have to use your gifts on others, but you could instead turn and use them on yourself. Which gifts would you use on yourself? How could you offer yourself the same support you offer others?

What can you regularly do for self-care that will honor your gifts?

What kind of creative activities can you do alone to honor your own value?

_____

_____

_____

_____

_____

What unique things about you begin to come out when you're alone or doing something just for yourself and your own enjoyment? What do you see that is just for you and not for others?

_____

_____

_____

_____

_____

The truth is that you cannot truly be of lasting service to others until you are of service to yourself. The true gift of being an empath is not in your connection to others, but in your connection to yourself as a powerful and liberated force of nature.

Your gifts do not make you a sacrificial lamb. Your sensitivity does not make you a martyr. You are more than that. If you deny yourself your autonomy, you deny the world what it truly needs: you.

What Drains You vs. What Fills You Up

Knowing when your cup is empty and when your cup is full tells you exactly how to shift and prioritize your boundaries. If you are honest about where you are, and are aware of the people and situations that tend to drain you and the people and situations that fill you up, being fluid with your boundaries becomes that much easier.

Take stock of the people who drain you, the places that drain you, and the tasks that drain you. List all the things that tend to suck the energy from you.

Take stock of the people and places and situations that bring you joy and energize you and fill you up. List all the things that tend to fill your cup and bring you happiness.

- _____
- _____
- _____
- _____
- _____
- _____
- _____
- _____
- _____
- _____
- _____

- _____
- _____
- _____
- _____
- _____
- _____
- _____
- _____
- _____
- _____
- _____

You will have different levels of energy and availability all the time. Knowing what drains you and what fills you up can help you examine where you are at any given time so you can make better choices for yourself as you go along. For example, if you already know you are feeling exhausted and drained, you may want to avoid certain people on your "people who drain you" list, or say "no" when someone asks you to take on too many draining tasks. You may also know to turn to the things that fill you up when you're feeling drained.

On the other hand, when you know you are feeling full and satisfied, you may have more availability to help others and take things on. Every choice you make is an opportunity to practice your boundaries and respect what you need.

In what ways have you not been honoring your energy levels and boundaries lately?

_____

_____

_____

_____

Seeing how quickly your emotional energy changes, how can you use this information to shift the way you use your boundaries?

_____

_____

_____

Pick three of the things from your "things that drain you" list, and commit to avoiding them next time you are already feeling drained.

1._____

2._____

3._____

Because verbal expression of boundaries is so important, write down what you would say to someone who asks you to take on more than you can handle when you are already feeling drained. Practice speaking it out loud.

_____

_____

_____

_____

In what ways have you been honoring your energy levels and boundaries lately?

_____

_____

_____

_____

Pick three of the things from your "things that fill you up" list that you will commit to in order to continue honoring those boundaries.

1. _____

2. _____

3. _____

Letting Go of Expectations

Being able to honor your own boundaries is a huge victory. Stepping up and expressing what you need changes the quality of your entire life. What happens, though, when you don't ultimately get what you want after you express your boundaries?

Boundaries are not necessarily about other people. Even though boundaries often involve the behavior of others, you cannot put boundaries on what someone else is allowed or not allowed to do or say. The important distinction here is that your boundaries are about *you*: you are making clear what kind of behavior and communication you will personally allow in your life—and you cannot have expectations on how the other person will react.

If the other person chooses to respect your boundaries and work with you on certain behaviors, that's wonderful. But you cannot express boundaries only as a way to force people to change. You can only decide what conditions are needed for you to continue a relationship, and if those conditions aren't met, it's up to you to let go and move on in order to stay true to your own boundaries. You are making choices with your boundaries, and you need to let others make their own choices as well.

Describe a relationship where there was a struggle around your boundaries. Which boundaries were not respected?

Looking back, what expectations did you have of the other person when you expressed your boundaries?

_____

_____

_____

_____

How did that relationship pan out?

_____

_____

The unfortunate truth is that the clearer you become about your boundaries, the more likely it is that many people and situations will fall away. Not everyone is ready to work with you. Sometimes, your boundaries will be very different from the boundaries of the other person, and you need to respect theirs as well. If your only desired outcome is to change the other person, you will probably be very disappointed, as expecting others to change simply because you're changing is a fool's errand. Your primary goal here is only to change yourself and the conditions you choose to live in. Those who stay to work with you are a welcome bonus.

The silver lining, however, is that when you habitually stay true to yourself and your boundaries and needs, you will only let people in if they are on the same page as you. You will have a screening process for every relationship and every situation—which, granted, kicks a lot of things off the radar, but it also lets in up-leveled relationships that focus on respect and authenticity.

Describe a time when you went back on your boundaries because the other person didn't want to engage with them. What happened and how did it make you feel?

Describe a relationship where the other person wanted to work with you on your boundaries and put in a real effort to change the way they behaved or communicated with you. How did that make you feel?

Describe a relationship where the other person expressed boundaries to you that you did not want to engage with. What happened?

Describe a relationship where the other person expressed their boundaries and you chose to change the way you communicated or behaved with them. What happened and how did that make you feel?

Describe a relationship where the other person had vastly different and conflicting boundaries from yours. What happened?

Describe a relationship you had to let go of to respect yourself and your boundaries. How did that affect you? What was the quality of your life after that?

Look at all the varied experiences and relationships you just wrote about. This should illuminate how nuanced and complicated working with boundaries can be. Boundaries are not simply things that are set in stone. They are choices. Numerous choices that both you and the other person need to make time and time again. No matter the complications, though, letting go of expectations and following your values and your integrity will ultimately lead you in the right direction. Making good choices for your own life might not always feel good, but it always feels right.

CHAPTER 6

Relationships

IF YOU REALLY WANT TO CHECK AND SEE HOW YOU'RE HANDLING YOUR EMPATH NATURE, JUST LOOK AT YOUR RELATIONSHIPS. Relationships, whether romantic, platonic, or familial, are the playground for almost every joyful and painful aspect of the unique empath system. In many ways, these relationships are often the quickest and clearest teachers when it comes to your wounds, triggers, gifts, and insecurities, which is why it's so important to constantly work on being your most authentic and empowered self with others.

Because of your sensitivities, you may have found that attracting or keeping healthy relationships has been especially difficult for you, more so than for other people. By exploring your relationships, past and present, you will be empowered to create healthy dynamics and patterns, which will help you release relationships that are no longer good for you, improve the relationships you want to keep, and attract new relationships that will be a better fit for you.

You'll notice in this section that the exercises and prompts cover a wide variety of relationship dynamics, including dating, relationship growth, and breakups. Because of that, you may not immediately identify with each one. Feel free to skip the prompts that don't apply to you. You can also modify them to fit your own relationships. For example, if you're single, you can still use the romantic relationship prompts by calling upon your romantic history, discovering past histories and patterns for you to look at. You may also find that different people in your life fit multiple relationship patterns, whether romantic, platonic, or familial.

Make a list of the most important relationships (family, friends, romantic partners, business partners) in your life. Include past relationships that were especially significant.

- _____
- _____
- _____
- _____
- _____
- _____

- _____
- _____
- _____
- _____
- _____
- _____

Looking at your list, pick the relationship you feel is/was the healthiest or happiest. What kind of positive patterns and communication are/were involved that make it feel healthy?

_____

_____

Now pick the relationship you feel is/was the most unhealthy or toxic. What kind of negative patterns and communication are/were involved that make it feel unhealthy?

Pick one relationship you're currently still in where one or both of you are working on improving the relationship. What is helping? What obstacles are you facing?

Relationship Patterns

Identifying common relationship patterns that empaths fall into will illuminate the obstacles you're experiencing and help you break those patterns to create something healthier and more sustainable.

WHOSE ENERGY IS WHOSE?

One of the biggest struggles for empaths is feeling overwhelmed by energies and emotions to the point where you can't tell where you stop and someone else begins. Maybe you're feeling sad, and you don't know if you're actually sad or if you're feeling the sadness of the person you're with. Or, on the flip side, maybe you're feeling angry about something someone said and lashing out at that person, when really, it was your own energy from a past wound you were feeling. It can be really confusing to parse out where certain feelings come from when you can feel so many things at once. Usually, this confusion is a combination of the effects of your sensitivity and having boundaries that are not working for you—or not having boundaries at all. Because of this, both your environment and a self-examination of your boundaries must be accounted for when you're trying to figure the energies out.

In what relationships and situations do you tend to get the energies confused the most?

_____

_____

_____

_____

What are the negative consequences you've experienced as a result of not being able to discern your energies from those of others?

Have you noticed any environmental factors that tend to be present when this happens? If so, what are they? A lot of empaths also have sensory issues and may notice extra confusion when experiencing sensory overwhelm, like too much background noise or too many people around.

How can you change your environment when you're feeling confused about energies?

Check your boundaries. How are they in the relationships and situations where you get confused about energies the most?

_____

_____

_____

_____

How can you change your boundaries when you're feeling confused about energies?

_____

_____

_____

_____

The easiest way to begin to separate your energies from someone else's is to create an actual, physical separation. Give yourself space. Turn your phone off and take a communication break. Go on solo walks in nature. Take salt baths and burn herbs to smoke cleanse your energy field. Do whatever you can to create actual space between yourself and those people and situations, and let their influence fall away as you refocus on your self-awareness practices, like writing in this guided journal.

THE ACCOMMODATION CHAMELEON

Because empaths are so sensitive to the unspoken emotional needs of others, this can make them especially helpful under the right circumstances. You may be able to feel what someone needs before they even feel it themselves. It's a magical gift of emotional anticipation, right? When you're that tuned in, you actually have the ability to alter your actions or approach in order to help others.

Describe a time when you could intuitively feel what someone else needed before they told you. What were their needs, and how could you help them in that instance?

_____

_____

_____

_____

_____

Describe a time when you happily dampened a certain part of your personality or exaggerated another part of your personality in order to keep the peace or make others feel good.

_____

_____

_____

Think about and describe a current circumstance in your life where you receive positive benefits and avoid negative consequences by changing or hiding parts of your personality for others. (For example, this pattern is often necessary in work or professional environments, or even in dangerous situations where your reaction may create negative results.)

_____

_____

_____

_____

Like all empath gifts, the accommodation chameleon pattern has its dark side as well. While putting others before yourself sometimes is a kind and generous thing to do, it's not something that you should do every time. If you are so tuned into someone else's emotional needs, and you tend to have a people-pleasing pattern, this gift can cause you to willingly change your identity or personality on a regular basis just to make things better or easier for others. While a few isolated incidents of this are fine (think of them as little white lies), if you do it over and over again, you'll begin to lose sight of your authentic personality. Eventually, it will feel like you have to play pretend with the people you love. Then, that will connect back to your core wound and make you feel more and more unseen and lonely.

It's common for empaths to change their personality for the sake of others, especially family members, and even more so if the empath is the black sheep of the family. Other times, this type of change is present in romantic relationships or friendships. Whatever the case, though, it's usually the same people that consistently bring out this side of the empath.

List a few of the people in your life that experience your accommodation chameleon pattern the most. What aspects of yourself do you change, silence, or amplify in order to please them?

How do they feel whenever you do this? How do you feel whenever you do this?

How long have you been doing this, and what would happen if you stopped?

Is it worth it to stop doing this and be unapologetically yourself with them? Why or why not? There is no wrong answer to this question, and you'll find that the answer often changes with time and circumstances.

PARENTIFICATION

Parentification occurs when a child is put in a position where they are responsible for some or all of the duties of a parent. These duties can be physical responsibilities, such as cooking, cleaning, and caretaking, especially if one or both parents are absent. But they can also be emotional responsibilities, like serving as an emotional support and confidant to a parent, and being exposed to much more adult trauma and confusion than is appropriate for their age. When parentification happens, children grow up way too fast and carry this heavy burden of responsibility into their adult years. Because of the naturally nurturing systems of the empath, parentification is all too common for empaths in their younger years, which creates a foundation of overwhelm and sucks out the joy of their childhoods. If you experienced this, it may also be connected to your core wound and the soul loss that occurred, in which case reconnecting with your inner child—and allowing them to be a child—will be especially healing.

Were you parentified as a child? If so, which duties or responsibilities fell on you?

Looking back, how did that affect your childhood and how you grew up? Did it affect the way you saw the world, your relationships with others, or how you saw yourself?

_____

_____

_____

_____

Which of those tendencies did you bring into adulthood? Do they affect your relationships now? (For example, maybe you automatically take up the mother role in relationships, and that causes those relationships to be imbalanced or unfulfilling.)

_____

_____

_____

_____

How can you bring more balance into those relationships, and how can you engage with your inner child to help?

_____

_____

_____

_____

CODEPENDENCY

As an empath, you know how easily the energies and emotions of other people affect you. When someone close to you is full of joy, that joy is contagious, and you feel it as well. When they're sad or angry, their emotions can immediately bring you down into those emotional spaces as well. While that level of feeling is a gift and a skill, these experiences also throw off the way you experience and receive validation. By allowing another person's emotions to be more present and more important than your own, you are training your sensitive system not only to match other people's, but also to look to others to tell you whether to feel good or bad. Your system begins to believe that you need another person to be happy in order for you to be happy. This process can result in a relationship addiction for the empath, where the empath constantly requires that hit of positive emotion from the other person in order to be okay. As you can imagine, this is a slippery slope into people-pleasing and codependency and loss of identity, which not only harms you, but the other person as well.

Which relationships in your life do you feel codependent in, past or present? How did/do the other person's emotions tend to decide what yours are?

In what ways did your behavior change so you could help prevent the other person (and yourself) from experiencing negative emotions?

_____

_____

_____

If you didn't have to worry about how others felt or what you needed to do for them, what would you be like?

_____

_____

_____

If you didn't need validation from anyone else, if your feelings did not depend on anyone else's feelings, what would your ideal life look like?

_____

_____

_____

_____

_____

EMOTIONAL LABOR

A common pattern for empaths is taking on an imbalanced amount of emotional labor in their relationships. Emotional labor is the work a person puts in to hold space for and process the emotions of others. It's also the tasks automatically given to the person who tends to be the nurturer, like remembering birthdays, planning get-togethers, and handling phone calls with friends or family who are struggling.

What kind of emotional labor have you been expected to put in for your loved ones?

Do you feel appreciated for all of the emotional labor you do? Why or why not?

What would happen if you stopped putting in more emotional labor than you can handle?

_____

_____

_____

You may expect pushback from others if you consciously lessen the amount of emotional labor you do. Other people might simply be used to the space you hold and the tasks you accomplish. Communicating about this imbalance with others, however, may help you lighten the load and balance the labor with their support.

How can you communicate with your loved ones so they might understand the emotional labor you do? What would you ask them to do so you can feel less overwhelmed?

_____

_____

_____

_____

_____

_____

_____

ABUSIVE RELATIONSHIPS AND GASLIGHTING

It can be common for empaths to fall into abusive relationships. When you are feeling overwhelmed by emotions and energy, and have trouble discerning what is yours and what is everyone else's, that creates a vulnerability—an opening for people to come in and decide for you. Many empaths have histories of trauma and abuse as well, which can keep the empath disempowered, and also make it harder for them to break out of old, destructive habits and perspectives—which, in turn, means it's easier for them to fall back into those patterns with other abusers.

Do you have a history of abuse or trauma? If so, which of those wounds or negative patterns do you still feel stuck in or endangered by?

If you have experienced multiple abusive relationships in your life, what are the shared patterns or behaviors from those relationships that you can see clearly now?

Knowing what you know about yourself now, what advice would you give yourself to either get out of an abusive situation or avoid one in the future?

Gaslighting is a manipulation tactic often used in abusive dynamics to plant seeds of doubt in the victim, making them question their own sanity. While those who gaslight will often use lying as a tactic, gaslighting is different from lying in that its goal is not just to change the facts, but to shift the blame onto the other person and manipulate them into thinking, feeling, and acting differently. If you're already confused and overwhelmed by out-of-control empathy, you are especially susceptible to gaslighting, because you are more willing to accept someone else's reality over yours.

Who in your life has gaslit you? What were the circumstances and what did they make you question about yourself?

How did you get out of that situation?

Knowing what you know about yourself now, what advice would you give to yourself to prevent it from happening again?

If you're unsure of whether a relationship you're in crosses the line into abuse, here is a checklist of red flags to look out for. Keep in mind that one problematic behavior does not automatically mean the relationship is abusive, as we are all problematic at times, but allow yourself to see the overall picture and honestly look at how safe you are in the relationship.

IN AN ABUSIVE RELATIONSHIP, THE OTHER PERSON OFTEN:

- Moves too fast in the relationship, starting it with an excess of flattery, gifts, and planning (also known as love bombing)

- Is controlling of the way you spend your time and who you spend it with, to the point of isolating you from your loved ones and hobbies

- Has narcissistic traits and tendencies

- Criticizes you excessively

- Uses the phrase "No one else would ever love you"

- Doesn't take responsibility for their actions or behaviors

- Is very jealous, even accusing you of cheating (this can often be a sign that they are the one being unfaithful)

- Has a rocky relationship history, blaming each relationship failure on their exes, often saying their exes were "crazy"

- Doesn't respect your boundaries, may cross them intentionally

- Has an out-of-control temper with you, but seems to be even-tempered, even charming, with others

- Uses the silent treatment or ignoring you as a punishment

- Controls or wants to control your finances

- May have a history of being abused themselves

- Throws items when angry (this is often the precursor to physical violence)

- Acts out any kind of physical or sexual violence

If you checked too many of those boxes, and you are in any type of danger in your relationship, you need to leave. Abusive relationships do not improve, and even if your empath nature makes you want to excuse the bad behavior or change the person because you love them, you deserve better and need to get out immediately. Talk to friends and family and come up with a plan. Your beautiful soul and sensitivity deserve healing and compassion away from abusive dynamics.

Safety

This may not seem like the most surprising thing to hear, but having a foundation of safety is necessary for any and all sustainable growth in any relationship. This includes physical safety, of course, but also emotional safety, which is paramount for an empath, who has *so many* emotions. You know you have emotional safety in a relationship when you feel safe expressing yourself and your feelings to the other person. This includes expressing points of conflict or issues that have come up. It's never easy to express conflict, but knowing the other person will listen to you and communicate with you is what creates that safety and intimacy.

The biggest indication that you're lacking safety in any relationship is the feeling that you're constantly walking on eggshells. Describe the relationships that make you feel this way.

What has happened in the past to make you walk on eggshells? What are you afraid will happen?

_____

_____

_____

_____

_____

_____

When someone repeatedly makes you feel this way or has been shown to destroy safety with their actions or words, it's often an indication that it's time to release that relationship. What relationships have you already released because of this, and which ones do you already know you need to release now?

_____

_____

_____

_____

As such a sensitive being, it might be scary to ask for emotional safety. Sometimes, we may perceive someone's lack of emotional safety with us, but we haven't yet done the work of communicating our own needs and boundaries. Being able to communicate your needs might completely change the tides, as even the idea of emotional safety may be foreign to others, and they may need a little help too.

Who have you not clearly communicated your needs and boundaries to? Why not?

Practice what you would say. Write those needs here and practice speaking them out loud.

Dating as an Empath

Dating as an empath can be a minefield of complications. Beyond the fact that it's simply an overstimulating process for the highly sensitive person, with all the apps and the chatting and the meeting in crowded places and the taking in everyone's energies, dating is also where you will immediately test your boundaries and patterns. The good news is that even your worst dates can teach you so much about yourself and strengthen your own convictions. Not to mention, the stronger you feel in yourself and the more aware you are of both yourself and the other person, the more likely it is you'll find someone wonderfully compatible with you—someone who loves you for you.

TRAUMA BONDING

One of the tendencies you need to be aware of as an empath dating is trauma bonding. Empaths tend to engage in trauma bonding more than others, even if it's not consciously done. Because you're an empath, others tend to open up to you very quickly, sharing their wounds or trauma. And because you're an empath, being seen in your own trauma is a very validating experience. This perfect storm can cause the both of you to develop a strong and immediate intimacy over sharing trauma. Even though bonding over your struggles is a normal and healthy thing, if it happens in this context too early, it can also create relationship patterns and roles that offset the balance of the relationship before it even starts. You may find yourself taking on a therapist or caretaker role for the other person, and you may also associate intimacy with trauma, subconsciously stirring up that bond based on trauma to create more intimacy and connection.

Describe a relationship that began or developed with trauma bonding.

How did that relationship progress? If it ended, how did it end?

Looking back, were the roles you played for one another inappropriate for a sustainable and lasting relationship? If yes, how so?

_____

_____

_____

_____

_____

_____

What can you do when starting a relationship to increase intimacy without relying on trauma bonding?

_____

_____

_____

_____

_____

_____

_____

PARENTING YOUR PARTNER

While parentification often happens when someone is treated like a parent when they're a child, that experience can often form a vicious cycle where the empath continues that learned pattern in romantic relationships. You may step into the role of caretaker for your partner, and in a way, almost manage and control the relationship like a parent might with their child. Whether consciously or unconsciously, parenting your partner may be helpful in small doses, but having that dynamic as a large part of your relationship can often lead to burnout, resentment, and diminished attraction.

A less obvious version of this dynamic is attempting to fulfill the neglected needs of your partner in an unbalanced way. For example, let's say your new partner has confided in you the things they didn't receive from their parents or their previous partners. Because you can feel their pain and want them to be happy, you may jump into caretaking mode to attempt to make up for all of those neglected needs as soon as possible. Fulfilling and nurturing your partner's needs is a wonderful thing, but when taken to the extreme, as empaths often do, this is where the empath loses their own identity and autonomy in the process, leading straight back to those patterns of people-pleasing, parentification, and codependency.

Describe a relationship where you ended up in the role of the other person's parent instead of their partner.

Looking back, can you pinpoint the time period or circumstance where you crossed the line from a helpful partner into the parental role? Take an honest inventory and describe those circumstances.

Did you have a partner who didn't want you to step out of that caretaking role for them? What happened?

How can you respond differently in your current or future relationships to avoid crossing this line?

RED FLAGS

Here are some of the common red flags and behaviors that empaths may be more susceptible to during dating. Use this checklist as an inventory when meeting new potential partners:

- **LOVE BOMBING.** This means coming on (too) strong in the very early stages with compliments, gifts, declarations of love, plans for the future, and so forth. Love bombing is almost a sure sign that the other person will either ghost you or use the love bombing phase to become more neglectful and potentially abusive later. Because of the patterns of codependency that many empaths have, you need to be especially honest with yourself about this one.

- **BREADCRUMBING.** Giving you just enough attention and affection to string you along without making any real commitments or showing up for any real intimacy.

- **DOESN'T RESPECT YOUR TIME OR SPACE.** Does your potential partner send you too many texts when they know you're busy? Do they try to pin down your location too often? Are they angry when you don't respond in the timeframe they desire? This may indicate future controlling behavior.

- **PUSHING YOUR CLEARLY STATED BOUNDARIES.** Does your potential partner know your boundaries around relationships and sex? If they do, and still continue to push the edges of your boundaries, even in a playful way, this is an immediate reason to end the relationship. Because empaths have such a difficult time with boundaries in the first place, anyone who is unhealthy for the strength of your boundaries from the beginning will not be good for you.

- **INABILITY TO COMMUNICATE THROUGH CONFLICT.** Does your potential partner respond negatively to any hint of conflict or tension in the early stages? If they respond with anger or avoidance instead of willingly communicating, this is a strong indicator that the relationship would not withstand the larger conflicts that come with sustainable partnership.

- **DATING FOR POTENTIAL.** Because empaths tend to be so sensitive to the hidden gifts of others, they often find themselves dating for their partner's potential. Are you seeing someone who you believe has a lot of potential and simply isn't showing up for it yet? Don't do it. Dating someone for their potential is the easiest way to allow yourself to slip into a caretaking or healer role instead of a partnership. Let people do their own self-work, and choose those who meet you where you are.

- **MIXED SIGNALS.** Do yourself a favor and just automatically assume that mixed signals mean no. If you are sensitive and are on a healing journey, the last thing you need is another rollercoaster of emotion to ride. Honor your own feelings and let other people sort out their own.

Recall any relationships you entered that had some of these red flags. What happened?

_____

_____

_____

_____

_____

_____

Knowing what you've learned about yourself since then, how can you avoid falling into those common traps?

_____

_____

_____

_____

When you're dating as an empath, you want to make sure you're not getting into a relationship (or situationship) that will just be confusing or a waste of your energy. By being clear about your values and needs, and being aware of the patterns to watch out for, you will bypass a lot of the potential relationships that aren't good for you, making more room for the wonderful people that will be compatible with your sensitive nature and your relationship goals.

Growing in Relationships as an Empath

When you're already in a relationship, you have a different set of experiences and obstacles to work with as an empath. The biggest consideration in a long-term relationship is to make sure that compatible growth is happening for both of you, as individuals and as a couple. As you grow and change over time, it's healthy to take inventories and reassess goals and issues as you go.

Take an inventory of your relationship. List the struggles and obstacles you have encountered in your relationship—the things that are preventing either individual or collective growth.

How many of those struggles are connected to core wounds, negative relationship patterns, or lackluster boundaries? Write them out, and if you can, list which known wounds and patterns are connected to the individual struggles.

Take an inventory of your relationship. List the ways your relationship is strong and healthy, the things that grow in your relationship as you both grow individually as well.

Which of those positive aspects of your relationship are there because of the healing work either of you have done? What kind of healing did you do?

COLLECTIVE AND INDIVIDUAL GROWTH

In any relationship, it's normal to have ups and downs, periods of mutual growth and periods of mismatched growth. We may take individual side roads in our growth apart from our partners, but the best partnerships will still ultimately grow in the same direction.

In what ways do you feel that your partner is growing in the same direction as you?

In what ways do you feel that you and your partner are growing in different directions?

Do you feel that you and your partner are able to come back together after you've grown in different directions, or that your relationship may not be able to withstand that kind of difference? Why?

When empaths are on healing journeys, their identities can often shift dramatically as they come to terms with their past and their pain. As an empath, do you find yourself shifting or changing quickly? What do you feel is changing?

How is your partner affected by your shifts and changes?

How does your partner support your growth?

How does your partner not support your growth?

Your partner may be benefiting from some of your empath patterns, like people-pleasing or caretaking. When you break those patterns for yourself, it can often be a moment of growth for your partner as well. Which patterns does your partner benefit from, and how are they handling you breaking those patterns?

As of this moment, do you believe you and your partner are growing sustainably together, or do you believe it's time to reassess the relationship?

TRIGGERS TO TRIGGER EACH OTHER

Sometimes, a really well-matched couple can have wounds that perfectly trigger each other's wounds. Maybe your partner provokes you, and then the way you respond to your own trigger ends up activating them, and then it's a whole chaotic chain of triggers that doesn't seem to end.

In what ways do your triggers actually trigger your partner, and vice versa?

What happens when both of you are triggered?

While this trigger effect can bring a lot of destruction, it also gives both of you a huge opportunity to communicate and heal together. If even one of you can start defusing triggers instead of getting carried away with them, it opens up a dialogue to get to the bottom of both of your wounds.

When your partner triggers you, what can you do instead of reacting to your trigger?

_____

_____

_____

_____

_____

When you trigger your partner, what can you do instead of reacting to their trigger?

_____

_____

_____

_____

_____

How does your core wound(s) relate to your partner's core wound(s)?

_____

_____

_____

_____

_____

What would happen to your relationship if you both could talk through these triggers and wounds instead of repeating the triggering process?

_____

_____

_____

_____

_____

_____

Being able to communicate with your partner about your wounds and triggers brings enough awareness into the relationship that when they come up again, you both have a better chance of approaching each other's triggers with compassion and neutrality, rather than arguments and defenses. Not only does that lessen the arguments, but it also adds an entirely new layer of intimacy into your love for you to enjoy.

ENERGETIC PRIVACY

It's not easy to be an empath. What's more, it's also not easy to be in a relationship with one. Sometimes the empath's ability to feel everyone's emotions and energies backfires on an intimate relationship. This can happen when your partner hasn't had the chance to go through and process their own feelings and energies. Their way of processing things is likely very different from yours and can take a lot longer if they're not being constantly bombarded with energy and feelings like you are. Because of this, you may often feel what's happening with your partner's emotions before they do. While you may think you're being helpful by verbalizing what you feel is happening with them before they tell you, it's not always a good idea. They need their own energetic privacy to figure out what's going on without you telling them, even if it's maddening for you to wait.

Describe a time when you knew what your partner was feeling or experiencing before they told you.

_____

_____

_____

_____

If you told them what they were feeling before they could tell you, how did they respond?

_____

_____

How is your partner's emotional processing different from yours?

_____

_____

_____

What are some ways you can give your partner energetic privacy in the relationship?

_____

_____

_____

_____

_____

Ethically speaking, if you know things about someone before they tell you, whether you're in a relationship or not, it's generally best to keep it to yourself. Unless you're in an environment where it's been asked for, offering information that wasn't offered to you first can be an invasion of another person's privacy and a disservice to their own healing process.

Keep in mind, though, that this ability, in the right environment, turns into an amazing gift. Some examples of this are when you're giving intuitive readings to others, when friends or loved ones ask you openly for advice or information, and when you're addressing business or creative matters instead of personal ones.

EXERCISE: GRATITUDE

It's so important to remain grateful and appreciative of the people closest to you, even and especially when you—or they—are struggling or reassessing things.

THINK OF YOUR PARTNER OR SOMEONE IMPORTANT IN YOUR LIFE. LIST FIFTEEN THINGS ABOUT THEM THAT YOU'RE GRATEFUL FOR.

1.

2.

3.

4.

5.

6.

7.

8.

9.

10.

11.

12.

13.

14.

15.

Empath Breakups

Breakups happen. You don't always have to consider breakups as relationship failures, though. When a relationship ends, it's often because one or both people grew so much that the relationship was no longer a suitable container for them. And in that way, the ending of a relationship can be a positive thing—a milestone of growth, regardless of how you feel about the other person.

Even in negative circumstances, you can celebrate your growth. For example, let's say the relationship ended because your partner was unfaithful to you. If that was something that crossed your boundaries, you can honor your choice to stay true to yourself by not being in that relationship anymore. That kind of authenticity, even through pain, is still growth.

Why was your breakup a positive thing? What kind of growth happened for either of you that made the relationship stop working?

How does that growth help you make decisions in your future relationships?

SEEKING COMFORT

One thing that empaths particularly struggle with during breakups is the sheer amount of pain they experience. When you're already sensitive to everyone and everything, a breakup is a big loss. It's grief. It's a death, while the person is still alive. Because of that pain, there is a tendency for empaths to want to seek comfort from the very person they're experiencing the pain from. Seeking comfort from the source, however, is generally not the healthiest choice to make, because it can confuse you and make you forget the reasons the breakup is happening in the first place.

Describe a time when you wanted to seek comfort from the same person/relationship that created the pain.

How did that urge set back your healing process?

Instead of seeking comfort from the source of the pain, how can you turn to your friends or other loved ones for comfort instead?

Being able to validate your own pain and hold yourself in it is such an important practice for the empath. How can you create comfort and validation for yourself, even in the midst of your pain?

EXERCISE: VALIDATION AFFIRMATIONS

One way to honor your path moving forward is by using some validation affirmations. These are simply two sentences. The first sentence is what you miss about the relationship or what about the relationship caused you pain. This sentence is to validate the pain you're experiencing in your breakup. The second sentence is a statement of hope and what you can do with your future now that you're not in that relationship anymore.

Here are two examples:

I miss that I was never alone at night and that someone was always there. I am now able to spend my time however I'd like to, without anyone telling me what to do.

I feel so crushed that they fell out of love with me and criticized me so much. I am now making more room for someone to come into my life who loves all of me.

WRITE A FEW FOR YOURSELF.

_____

_____

_____

_____

This practice allows for you to witness the reality of the pain you experience, while also helping you focus on the future at the same time.

WORKING ON YOURSELF

If you're going through a breakup right now and you're already working in this journal, congratulations! You're already doing one of the most important things to do after a breakup. Every practice here is going to help you parse through your past experiences and get to know yourself on deeper levels, which is exactly what's needed after a relationship ends.

It's also incredibly important to be doing this kind of work before jumping back into the dating pool. A lot of people jump back in too soon and end up bringing their personal and unresolved messes into other people's lives, which just breeds more confusion for everyone. By focusing on yourself first and becoming clear on your own boundaries and goals, you'll be able to enter the dating pool with more confidence and clarity when you're ready.

No matter where you stand in your relationships, no matter the kind of relationships they are, they will always be an integral part of your experience as an empath. You will always be able to reflect on your experiences and observe the patterns in both yourself and others to understand where and how we've been wounded, and where and how we can heal. And above all else, these observations will always point you back to the most important relationship you can have as an empath: your relationship with yourself.

Conclusion

YOU'VE TAKEN YOURSELF THROUGH SO MANY DIFFERENT LAYERS AND ASPECTS OF YOURSELF IN THIS JOURNAL, illuminating many years' worth of struggles and strengths in the unique story of your life. You've done what a lot of people will not do. You've taken honest inventories of the things that make you, you. Know that you can return to this work at any time. Each time you take yourself through deeper layers of healing as an empath, you will notice even more nuance with every experience you live.

While being an empath isn't all sunshine and rainbows, being able to sort through the shadow aspects of yourself as such a sensitive and intuitive being only makes your light brighter and your gift stronger. You may walk through the world a little differently, but knowing how to care for, understand, and protect your unique system makes the world feel a little less overwhelming and a little more beautiful in its emotional complexity. In your emotional complexity.

In what ways has being an empath been a gift to you in your past?

How is being an empath a gift to your future?

ORA NORTH is a spiritual teacher, witch, and mental health advocate. While very involved in the spiritual community, North does not subscribe to the "love and light" or "good vibes only" mentality that can often whitewash or bypass the very real struggles of the marginalized. Because of this, her focus is on shadow work, and promoting the acceptance and validation of all of our feelings—not just the positive ones—as tools for growth. She is author of *I Don't Want to Be an Empath Anymore* and *Mood Magick*.

Also by Ora North

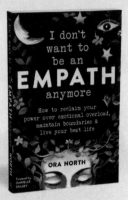

This guide offers practical exercises to help you navigate your intuition and empathic sensitivities, create much-needed boundaries with "energy vampires," build confidence, and stand strong in your power.

978-1684034178 / US $18.95

Packed with rituals and spells rooted in the elements, *Mood Magick* will help you navigate an ever-changing world with clarity and self-assurance.

978-1684038909 / US $16.95

🌿 **newharbinger**publications

◉ REVEAL PRESS

1-800-748-6273 / newharbinger.com